Contents

Introduction

These activity sheets are linked to the Big Books and provide reinforcement of the activities covered in the whole class session. They are in the same order as the Big Books and follow the requirements of the National Literacy Strategy.

Promoting independent working

If you are using *Ginn Big Book Phonics* in a Literacy Hour, the activity sheets can be used for independent group activities following the whole class focus. To make them useful for this purpose they have been designed to need a minimum of teacher input. Many follow a similar format to each other so the task may be quickly comprehended by the child.

Links to the Big Books

Some sheets provide a mini version of the Big Book, offering the child ownership of the Big Book text and then requiring work based on the Big Book page.

Tasks include:

- choosing between alternative spelling patterns
- reading a familiar text
- word building
- syllabification
- extended writing in different genres
- spelling activities
- joined handwriting of digraphs

Differentiation

Many of the activity sheets are in pairs covering the same topic. The first provides a first 'basic' visit to the task; the second a more challenging activity.

Activity Sheet 1

ay, ai and a-e

Name ______________________

Write. *ay* ______________________

Write. *ai* ______________________

Write the **ay** words on the haystack.

Write the **ai** words on the snail.

Write the **a-e** words on the cake.

Think of some more words with these spellings.
Write them with the others.

Write a sentence using some **ay**, **ai** or **a-e** words.

____

____

ay, ai and a-e

Activity Sheet 2

Name ______________________________

Finish the words with **ay**, **ai** or **a-e**.

1. I like to pl______ on the swings.
2. I eat my food off a pl______.

3. The snail leaves a tr______.

4. We put the cups on a tr______.

5. The dog wags its t______.

6. Mum had to t______ the cat to the vet.

7. I had seven candles on my birthday c______.

8. I take an umbrella in the r______.
9. I dig in the sand with a sp______.
10. There are seven d______ in a week.

Write a sentence using some **ay**, **ai** or **a-e** words.

____

____

Activity Sheet 3

ee and ea

Name ______________________

Write. ee ______________________

Write. ea ______________________

Write the **ee** words on the tree.

Write the **ea** words on the leaf.

Think of some more words with these spellings. Write them with the others.

Write a sentence using some **ee** or **ea** words.

____

ee and ea

Activity Sheet 4

Name ______________________________

Fill in the gaps with **ee** or **ea** words.

1. "Buzz buzz buzz," says the bumble ______.
2. I have ten toes on my ______.
3. On holiday I play in the sand on the ______.
4. You can swim in the ______.
5. Goldilocks met ______ bears.
6. I play with my friends in a football ______.
7. On hot days I like to eat ice ______.
8. I smell with my nose and I ______ with my eyes.
9. My teacher will ______ me to swim.
10. Lambs grow up to be ______.

Write a sentence using some **ee** or **ea** words.

____

Activity Sheet 5

y, ie and igh

Name ______________________________

Write. y ______________________________

Write. ie ______________________________

Write. igh ______________________________

Write the words on the right boxes.

y	ie	igh

Think of some more words with these spellings.

Write them on the right boxes.

Write a sentence using some **y**, **ie** or **igh** words.

____

____

y, ie and igh

Activity Sheet 6

Name ____________________________

Fill in the gaps with **y**, **igh** or **ie** words.

1. It is dark late at ______.
2. I eat cream with apple ______.
3. My dad wears a ______ round his neck.
4. My Mum wears ______ on her legs.
5. Birds ______ in the sky.
6. When I am sad I ______.
7. When I am tired I ______ on my bed.
8. My cat and my dog sometimes ______.
9. When there is no rain
   the flowers might ______.

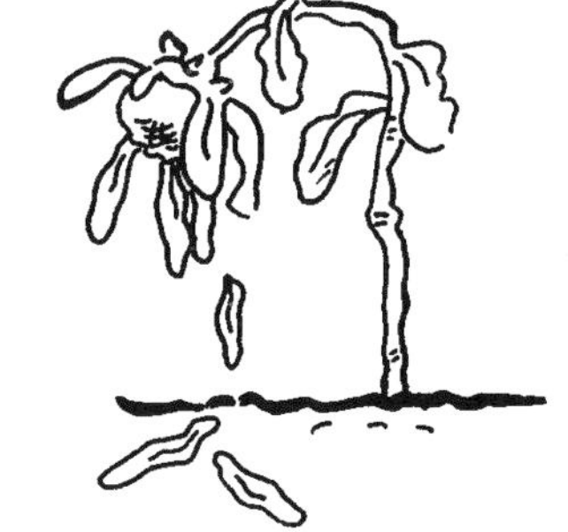

10. There are clouds in the ______.

Write a sentence using some **y**, **ie** or **igh** words.

____

____

Activity Sheet 7

i-e

Name ______________________________

Fill in the gaps with **i-e** words.

1. I like to ride on my ______.
2. I have ______ toes on my foot.
3. The bees are in the ______.
4. I like to play on the ______.
5. It is five o'clock, ______ for tea.
6. We play ______ and seek.
7. I had ten sweets but then I ate one.
   Now I have ______ sweets.
8. At the wedding the ______ wore a long dress.
9. The swimmers ______ into the pool.
10. I walk to school but some mums
    ______ their children to school.

Write a sentence using some **i-e** words.

____

ire and ile

Activity Sheet 8

Name ___________________________________

Finish the words with **ire** or **ile**.

1. The fire fighters put out the f____.
2. When I am happy I sm____.
3. On top of the church there is a sp____.
4. I go to sleep when I am t_____.

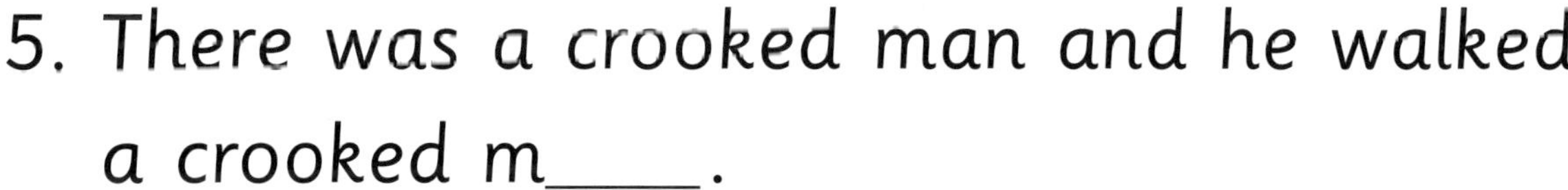

5. There was a crooked man and he walked a crooked m____.
6. The teacher keeps her papers in a f____.
7. The circus clown walked on the high w____.

8. All around the bath there are white t_____.
9. The teacher said, "Put your books on that p____."

Write a sentence using some **ire** or **ile** words.

____

____

Activity Sheet 9

ow, oa and o-e

Name ______________________________

Write. ow ______________________________

Write. oa ______________________________

Write the **ow** words on the bowl.

Write the **oa** words on the boat.

Write the **o-e** words on the phone box.

Think of some more words with these spellings.
Write them with the others.

Write a sentence using some **ow**, **oa** or **o-e** words.

____

oa and ow

Name ______________________

Activity Sheet 10

Fill in the gaps with **oa** or **ow** words.

1. I wash my face with _______ and water.
2. In the winter there is ice and _______.

3. A frog says, "Cr_____."
4. I cut a big slice of bread from the _______.
5. The footballer scored a _______.
6. If you plant a seed in the garden it will _______.

7. When it is cold I put on my hat and _______.
8. All around the castle there is a m_______.
9. I like to _______ snowballs at my friend.
10. I went to see a puppet _______.

Write a sentence using some **oa** or **ow** words.

____

____

Activity Sheet 11

ew and oo

Name ______________________________

Write. *ew* ______________________________

Write. *oo* ______________________________

Write the **ew** words on the stew pot.

Write the **oo** words on the moon.

Think of some more words with these spellings.
Write them with the others.

Write a sentence using some **ew** or **oo** words.

____

ew and oo crossword

Activity Sheet 12

Name ______________________________

Across

1. You see this in the sky at night.
4. Today the wind *blows*, yesterday it ________.
6. This is meat and vegetables cooked in a pot.
7. You go here to swim.

Down

2. You read this in the paper.
3. A pirate's gang is called the pirate's ________.
5. Spell pool backwards.

Write a sentence using some **ew** or **oo** words.

____

____

Activity Sheet 13

ue and u-e

Name ____________________

Fill in the gaps with a **ue** or a **u-e** word.

cute June tube tune

flute blue glue due Tuesday

1. The month after May is called ________.
2. I squeeze toothpaste out of a ________.

3. The puppy was little and ________.

4. I can play a ________ on my recorder.
5. I can play the recorder and the ________.

6. The sky is ________.
7. I stick things with ________.

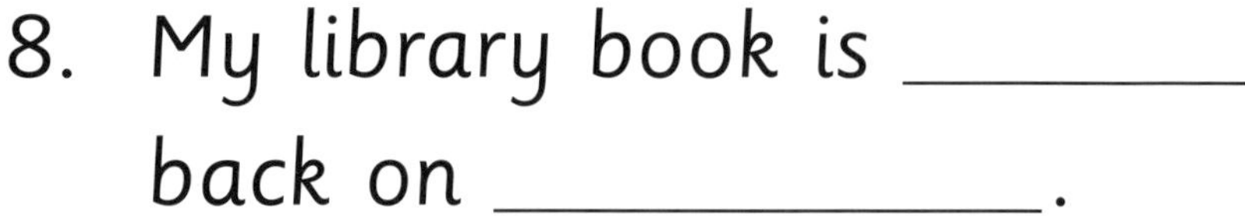

8. My library book is ________ back on ____________.

Write a sentence using some **ue** or **u-e** words.

____

____

ue and u-e wordsearch

Activity Sheet 14

Name ____________________

Spot the **ue** and the **u-e** words in the wordsearch.

a	k	c	u	t	e	m
w	c	h	z	q	x	o
f	l	u	t	e	y	c
r	u	t	u	b	e	u
u	e	e	r	l	t	b
d	n	s	t	u	n	e
e	g	l	u	e	v	p

tube

____

____

____

____

____

____

____

____

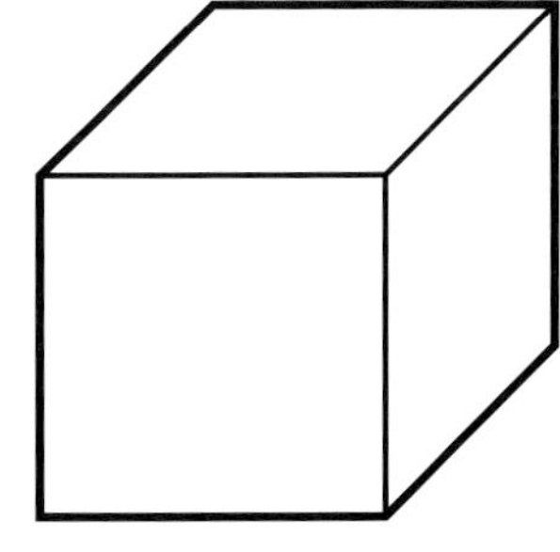

Write a sentence using some **ue** or **u-e** words.

____

Activity Sheet 15

Mark the Shark (ar)

Name ______________________

Write. ar ______________________

Fill in the gaps.

_______ the _______ is the deep sea _______,

He drives around in a dark blue _______.

His teeth are _______ and his suits are _______,

And his songs are top of the deep sea _______.

When he steps on the stage

in _______ Fish _______.

An _______ of fans shouts,

"We want _______!"

Write a sentence using some **ar** words.

____

____

ar

Name ______________________

Activity Sheet 16

Here are some **ar** words.

Mark Shark star car far park

dark bark cart start yard hard card

Use some of these words to help you to write your own poem or story about Mark the Shark.

Activity Sheet 17

ar

Name ____________________

Fill in the gaps with an **ar** word.

1. There are swings in the ________.
2. Mum drives the ________ to the shops.

3. We ________ school at 9 o'clock.
4. The cat can purr, but the dog can ________.
5. Help! I saw a ________ in the sea!

6. In the night sky we saw the moon and a ________.
7. At night it is ________.
8. In the snow I need a coat, a hat and a ________.

9. Cows, sheep and hens live on a ________.
10. On my birthday I got lots of ________ in the post.

Write a sentence using some **ar** words.

____

____

ar without the r

Activity Sheet 18

Name ____________________

How many **a** words can you find?
Make a list.

a	s	k	t	b	m	a	s	t
t	o	g	l	a	s	s	w	x
a	a	p	r	t	j	c	f	p
s	f	a	t	h	e	r	a	a
k	t	t	h	c	l	a	s	s
q	e	h	r	r	a	f	t	t
g	r	a	s	s	w	t	m	n

ask ____________________ ____________________

____________________ ____________________

____________________ ____________________

____________________ ____________________

____________________ ____________________

____________________ ____________________

Write a sentence using some **a** words from the wordsearch.

____

Activity Sheet 19	ow Name ____________________

Write. ow ____________________

Fill in the gaps.

Farmer ________ is ____________ ________.

His ________ is ____________,

His cats ________ - ________.

His duck goes ________,

His dogs ________,

So Farmer ________ is ____________ ________.

Write a sentence using some **ow** words.

____

____

ow

Name ________________________________

Activity Sheet 20

Fill in the gaps with **ow** words.

1. You can have a bath or a __________.

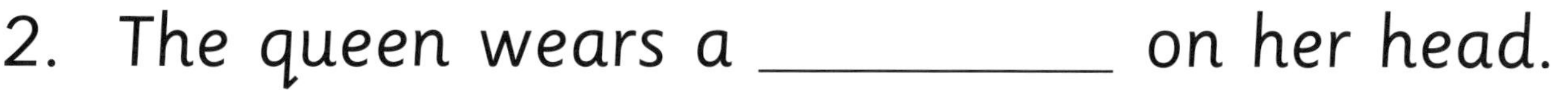

2. The queen wears a __________ on her head.

3. A ________ says, “Moo.”

4. You dry yourself with a __________.

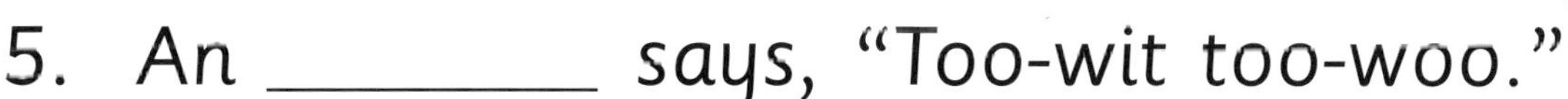

5. An ________ says, “Too-wit too-woo.”

6. A ________ has a big, red nose.

7. A dog says, “________ ________.”

8. When I hurt my knee I say, “________!”

9. There are lots of shops in the ________.

10. A ____________ grows in a garden.

Write a sentence using some **ow** words.

____

____

Activity Sheet 21

ou

Name ____________________

1. Write words that rhyme.

mouse ____________

pound ____________

loud ____________

fountain ____________

out ____________

2. Write the **ou** words to finish this little poem.

I saw a big black thunder ________,

And I heard the thunder, it was ________.

3. Use **ou** rhyming words to make up some little poems of your own.

ou and ow

Activity Sheet 22

Name ____________________

Write. ou ____________________

Write. ow ____________________

Write the **ou** words on the cloud.

Write the **ow** words on the cow.

Think of some more words with these spellings.
Write them with the others.

Write a sentence using some **ou** or **ow** words.

____

____

Activity Sheet 23

ow and ou

Name ______________________________

Fill in the gaps with an **ow** or **ou** word.

1. The __________ is happy.

2. The garden is full of __________.
3. We add some __________ to make a cake.

4. We went to the top of the __________.

5. We get milk from a __________.
6. The __________ hunts at night.

7. We splashed in the __________.
8. The mouse ran around the __________.
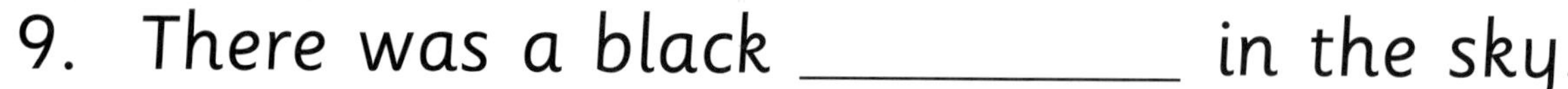
9. There was a black __________ in the sky.
10. Drums can make a very __________ sound.

Write a sentence using some **ow** or **ou** words.

____

____

Toys for the Boys (oy)

Activity Sheet 24

Name ______________________________

Write. oy ______________________________

Fill in the gaps.

Small ________, big ________, baby bath ________,

gold ________, old ________, make you laugh ________.

Good ________, bad ________, rather sad ________,

tall ________, small ________, jump for ________ ________.

How many **oy** words can you find? Make a list.

o	c	r	w	x	b	z
d	e	s	t	r	o	y
j	n	e	o	f	y	g
q	j	c	y	m	p	o
r	o	y	a	l	d	q
h	y	j	o	y	i	r

enjoy

____

____

____

____

____

Write a sentence using some **oy** words.

____

____

Activity Sheet 25

The Noisy Tortoise (oi)

Name ______________________________

Write. oi ______________________________

Fill in the gaps.

Avoid the ________ tortoise,

________ his noisy ________.

Avoid the noisy ________ –

it is the wisest ________.

He's a very ________ ________,

he ________ and shouts, "Oi! oi!"

and ________ and ________ and bounces

like a ________ squeaky toy.

Read the rhyme to your friends.

Write a sentence using some **oi** words.

____

oi wordsearch

Name ______________________

Activity Sheet 26

How many **oi** words can you find?

Make a list.

q	u	v	e	r	a	s	o	n
c	h	o	i	c	e	o	i	j
m	r	i	a	f	d	i	n	e
o	p	c	f	o	i	l	x	j
i	o	e	v	g	y	d	f	o
l	i	t	o	i	l	b	r	i
y	s	r	d	n	c	o	i	n
n	o	i	s	y	b	i	k	o
t	n	x	c	o	i	l	i	n

soil

____

____

____

____

____

____

____

____

____

Write a sentence using some **oi** words from the wordsearch.

____

____

Activity Sheet 27

oy and oi

Write the **oy** words on the oyster.

Write the **oi** words on the tortoise.

Think of some more words with these spellings. Write them with the others.

Write a sentence using some **oy** or **oi** words.

oi and oy crossword

Name ____________________________

Activity Sheet 28

	1			2			
3							
		4					5
6							
				7			

Across

1. If you break something, you __________ it.
4. We can plant a seed in this.
6. Another word for sound.
7. Children like to play with these.

Down

2. These pictures are on the door of the __________.

3. You can __________ to something with your finger.
5. Girls and ________ come out to play.

Write a sentence using some **oi** or **oy** words.

____

____

Activity Sheet 29

Red Riding Hood in the Woods

Name ___________________________

Write the labels.

Then write the story on the back of this page.

Wolf Story

Activity Sheet 30

Name ______________________

could would should put

push bush pull bull

Use some of these words to help you to write your own poem or story about a wolf.

Activity Sheet 31

Erk (er)

Name ______________________________

Look out for Erk!

Write about Erk.

Use as many **er** words as you can.

Urk (ur)

Activity Sheet 32

Name ____________________

Look out for Urk!

Write about Urk.

Use as many **ur** words as you can.

Activity Sheet 33

Irk (ir)

Name ____________________

Write about Irk.

Use as many **ir** words as you can.

Look out for Irk!

er, ir and ur wordsearch

Name ______________________________

Activity Sheet 34

How many **er**, **ir** and **ur** words can you find?

Make three lists.

v	c	o	w	l	f	i	r	s	t
h	e	r	b	v	h	k	s	a	h
k	z	a	i	b	d	u	l	f	i
a	r	x	f	k	g	y	t	e	r
r	h	m	s	o	i	x	u	r	t
h	a	l	h	e	r	a	r	n	y
g	e	m	x	r	l	m	k	m	t
j	d	t	e	a	c	h	e	r	b
f	h	u	r	t	g	k	y	m	i
i	x	r	b	u	r	n	b	h	r
x	w	n	u	r	s	e	s	t	d

er	ir	ur
herb	______	______
______	______	______
______	______	______
______	______	______

Write a sentence using some of the words you found in the wordsearch.

____

____

Activity Sheet 35

The Weekly Record (or)

Name ______________________

Write the report of storms in the north for The Weekly Record.

Use as many **or** words as you can.

STORMS IN THE NORTH

The Weekly Record (or)

Activity Sheet 36

Name ______________________________

Write about Gordon Stork and his horse.

Use as many **or** words as you can.

SPORTS REPORT
RECORD BROKEN

Activity Sheet 37

Astronaut and August crossword (au)

Name ____________________

1. Fit the **au** words into the astronaut crossword.

NAUGHTY

CAUGHT

AUTHOR

LAURA

A
S
T
R
O
N
A
U
T

2. Fit the **au** words into the August crossword.

PAUL

DAUGHTER

AUTUMN

A
U
G
U
S
T

Write a sentence using some **au** words from the crossword.

____

____

aw

Name ______________________

Activity Sheet 38

Fill in the gaps with the right **aw** word.

shawl lawn paws prawn straw
jaws crawl draw claws

1. You get a __________ with a carton of drink.
2. A ________ is made of grass.
3. Babies __________ before they walk.
4. A __________ is a sort of shellfish.

5. The old lady had a _________ round her shoulders.
6. I like to ________ and paint pictures.
7. Cats have __________ at the end of their __________.

8. When you chew food your ________ move.

Write a sentence using some **aw** words.

____

Activity Sheet 39

oor, or, aw and au

Name ____________________

Write **oor**, **or**, **aw** or **au** to finish the words.

1. Lions have sharp cl____s and strong j____s.
2. Close the d____r and sweep the fl____.
3. A h____se came round the c____ner.
4. ____gust is in summer, but October is in ____tumn.
5. The p____r old man lived in a shack on the m____r.
6. The teacher told us a st____y about a dark st____my night.
7. The baby cr____led on the l____n.
8. You cannot eat c____nflakes with a f____k.
9. Oops! Gordon has t____n his sh____ts!
10. The astron____t has a d____ghter called L____ra and a son called P____l.

Write a sentence using some **oor**, **or**, **aw** or **au** words.

____

In the Tooth Fairy's Lair (ai)

Activity Sheet 40

Name ______________________________

Write. *air* ______________________________

Fill in the gaps.

In the tooth ________ ________,

There are teeth all around.

Teeth on the ________,

Teeth on the ground.

Teeth on the ________,

Hanging in ________.

In the tooth ________ ________,

There are teeth all around.

Write a sentence using some **air** words.

____

____

Activity Sheet 41

air

Name ____________________

1. Fill in the gaps with an **air** word.
   Make a rhyme.

I saw a hairy ________. Then I saw three more.

There was one on the stair

and one on the ________

and one was flying in the ________.

2. Finish the sentences with an **air** word.

a) I need my ________ cut.

b) I went on lots of rides at the ________.

c) I gave my dad a ________ of slippers.

d) My brother said the tooth ________ gave him money for his tooth.

e) The dragon lives in a dragon's ________.

Write a sentence using some **air** words.

____

____

Beware of the Squares! (are)

Name ____________________

Activity Sheet 42

Write. *are* ____________________

Fill in the gaps.

If you land on a ________,

You will get a ________ ________.

There are bears there who ________,

There are ________ there who glare.

So ________! Take ________!

Do not dare, do not ________,

To land, to land, to land on a ________!

Write a sentence using some ***are*** words.

____

____

Activity Sheet 43

Scary bears

Name ____________________________________

dare scare spare care share

parent bare bear pair pear

Use some of these words to help you write your own poem or story about a scary bear.

are wordsearch

Name ________________________________

Activity Sheet 44

How many **are** words can you find?

Make a list.

s	j	s	k	v	b	s	m
t	d	c	j	r	e	h	j
a	f	a	p	s	d	a	j
r	a	r	e	p	a	r	m
e	b	e	w	a	r	e	q
s	q	u	a	r	e	x	t
c	a	r	e	e	h	v	b
c	i	y	m	k	c	m	c

stare

____

____

____

____

____

____

____

____

Write a sentence using an **are** word.

____

____

Activity Sheet 45

Same sounds, different spellings

Name ____________________

Draw pictures to show the difference between the words.

bare bear

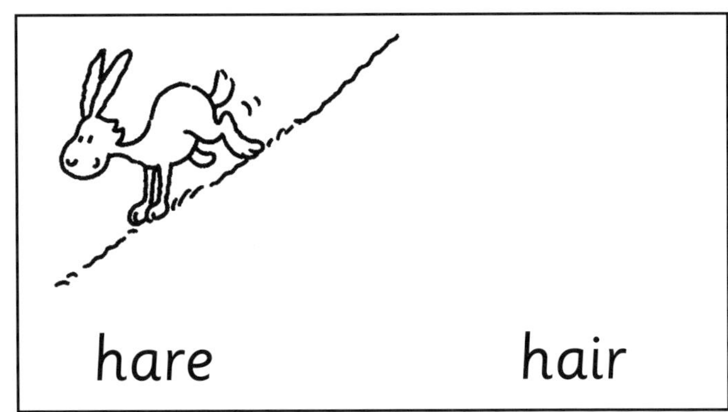

hare hair

stare stair

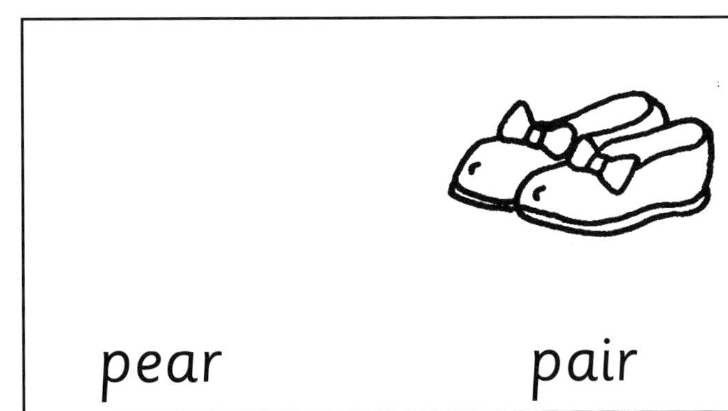

pear pair

Make up silly sentences using these words.

bear and bare
hare and hair
stare and stair
pair and pear

1. ____________________

2. ____________________

3. ____________________

4. ____________________

Picture Postcard (compound words)

Activity Sheet 46

Name ______________________________

Write the word in the gap under the picture.

Dear Gran,

Yesterday we went to the ______________. It was cool!

There was a ______________ with 300 steps! Afterwards

we walked along by the sea and I saw a ______________.

We found a cave and played at being ______________.

Then it started to rain – so I'm glad you packed my

______________.

Emma hasn't been so lucky. She has lost her

______________ so she has had to buy a new

______________ and a ______________.

She didn't have a ______________ so she got soaked!

Love, Tom

Activity Sheet 47

Puzzle page (compound words)

Name ____________________

Can you guess the words?

1. goldfish

2. ____________

3. ____________

4. ____________

Draw the two pictures that make the word.

snowman

pancake

handbag

bookcase

Write a sentence using one of the words in the pictures.

____

The Calender Rap

Activity Sheet 48

Name ____________________

Write one syllable in each bubble to write the names of the months.

1.
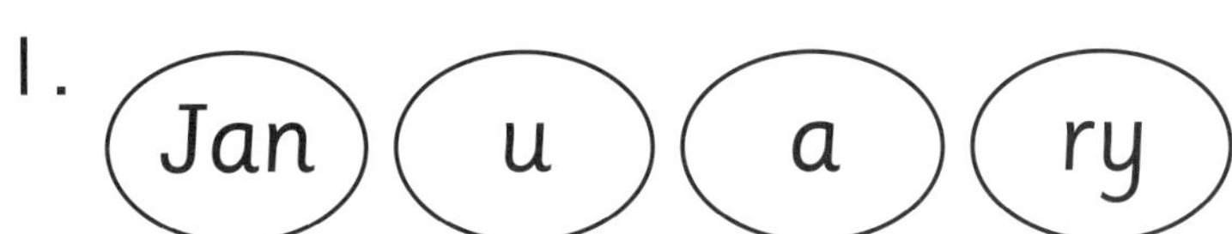

2.

3.

4.
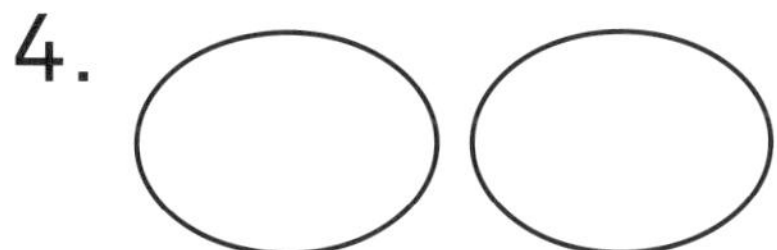

5.

6.

7.
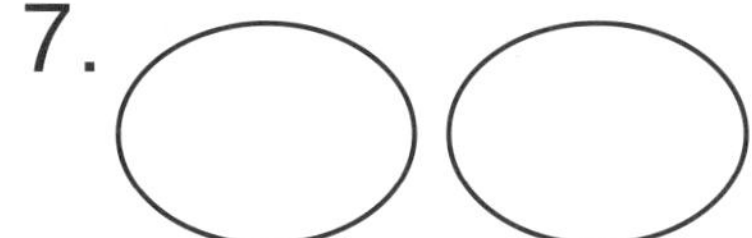

8.
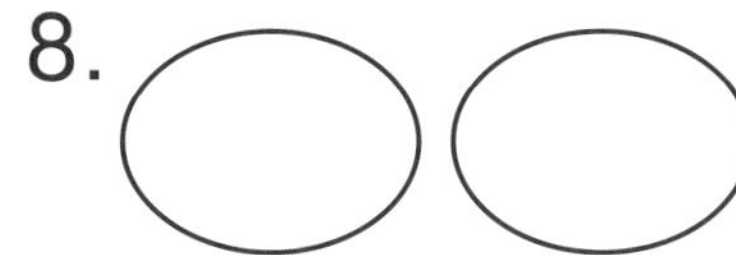

9.
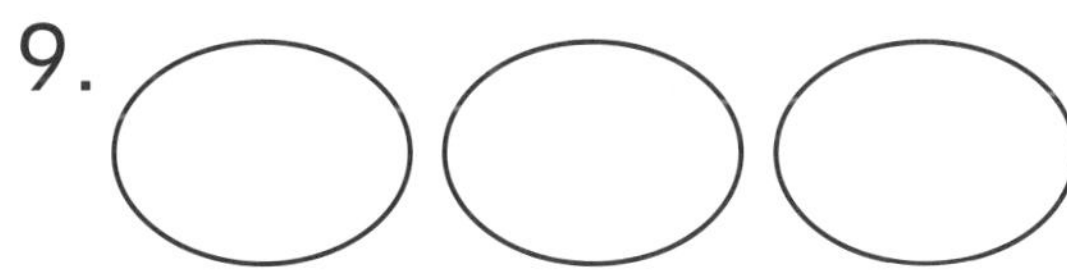

10.
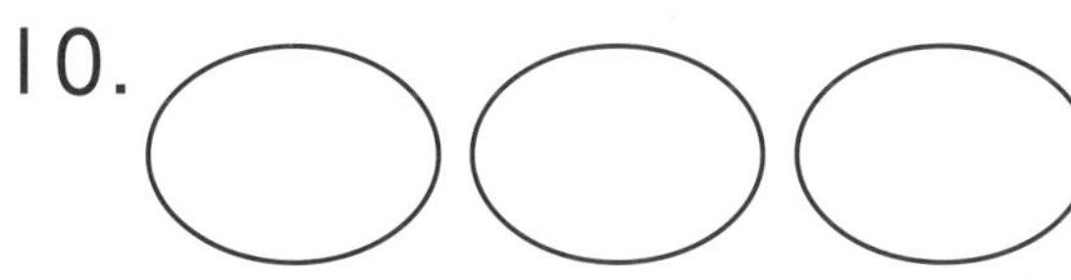

11.
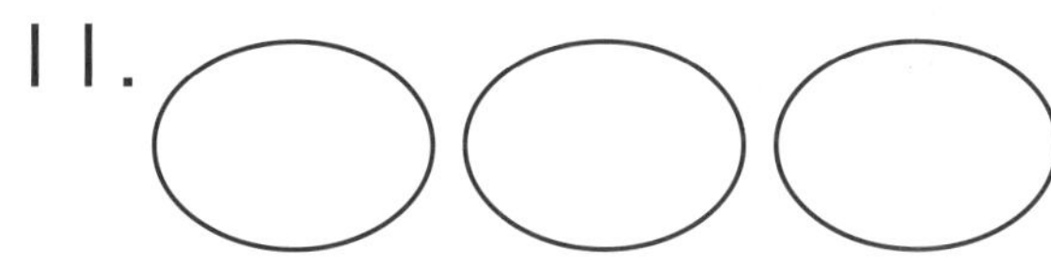

12.
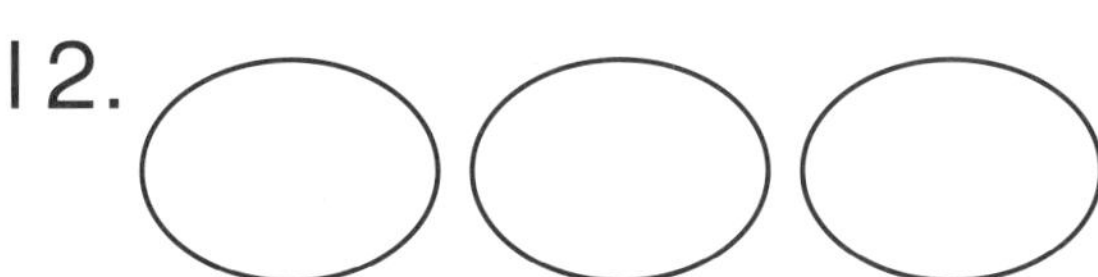

Put a ring round your birthday month.

Write a sentence using one of the names of the months.

____

____

Activity Sheet 49

Put it in order

Name ______________________________

Write the months of the year in order. Start with January.

1. ____________________ 7. ____________________

2. ____________________ 8. ____________________

3. ____________________ 9. ____________________

4. ____________________ 10. ____________________

5. ____________________ 11. ____________________

6. ____________________ 12. ____________________

Put the days of the week in order. Start with Monday.

1. ____________________ 5. ____________________

2. ____________________ 6. ____________________

3. ____________________ 7. ____________________

4. ____________________

Put the seasons in order. Start with Spring.

1. ____________________ 3. ____________________

2. ____________________ 4. ____________________

Syllables

Activity Sheet 50

Name ______________________________

Circle the syllables.

Mon day   zip   cow

Saturday   sheep   crocodile

lollipop   fatter   kitten

Write the words in the right boxes.

1	2	3
one-syllable words	two-syllable words	three-syllable words
cow	Monday	crocodile

Write a sentence using a one-syllable word.
Write a sentence using a two-syllable word.
Write a sentence using a three-syllable word.

Activity Sheet 51

Prefix un

Name ______________________________

1. Write **un** in front of these words to make new words.

____happy ____dress ____tidy ____zip

____pack ____fair ____true

2. Use the words you have made to finish these sentences.

a) Mum said my room was ______________.

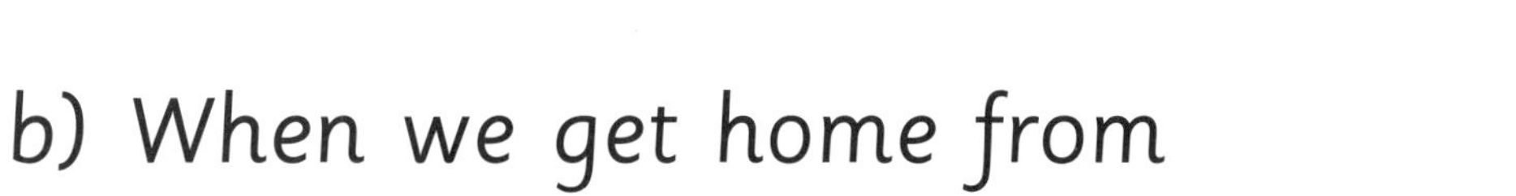

b) When we get home from holiday we ______________ our cases.

c) The baby cries when he is ______________.

d) A lie is ______________.

e) You have to ______________ before you go to bed.

f) I cannot ______________ my coat because it is broken.

g) Cheating is ______________.

3. Write a sentence using a word with an **un** prefix.

____

____

The wh quiz

Name ______________________________

Activity Sheet 52

Write the best **wh** question word in the gap. Then answer the questions.

What When Why Where Which

1. ________ were you born?

   ______________________.

2. ________ colour is your hair?

   ______________________.

3. ________ do you live? ______________________.

4. ________ is your favourite colour?

   ______________________.

5. ________ are you smiling?

   ______________________.

7. ________ do you like best? Sweets or chocolate?

   ______________________.

8. ________ is the dog?

   ______________________.

Write a question using a **wh** word.

____

Activity Sheet 53

ph and ch crossword

Name ____________________

All the answers are **ph** and **ch** words.
Write them in.

Across

2. 

4. A sound that comes back.

5. 

6. December 25th is ________.

Down

1. We go here to learn.

3. 

Write a sentence using some **ph** or **ch** words.

____

I Hear with my Little Ear

Activity Sheet 54

Name ____________________________________

Write. ear ____________________________________

Fill in the gaps.

I ________ with my little ________,

A buzz, buzz, buzz and it's very ________.

I ________ with my little ________,

A buzz, buzz, buzz and now – oh ________!

There's a great, big bumble bee stuck in my ________!

Write a sentence using some **ear** words.

____

____

Activity Sheet 55

ear wordsearch

Name ____________________

How many **ear** words can you find?
Make a list.

o	x	l	c	t	e	a	r	s
y	e	m	l	q	j	x	h	e
o	w	y	e	a	r	t	e	a
d	i	s	a	p	p	e	a	r
e	m	c	r	p	x	n	r	t
a	j	w	x	e	l	r	k	m
r	y	n	e	a	r	x	f	x
k	f	e	a	r	z	i	e	z

tears

Write a sentence using one of the words you have found in the wordsearch.

Bed and Jam

Name ______________________________

Activity Sheet 56

Write. ea ______________________________

Fill in the gaps.

Bread and jam, bread and jam,

_______ and jam in _______.

_______ _______ on the _______ spread,

and _______ _______ on my _______.

Jam _______ on the bed _______,

made it go bright _______!

Bread and jam, _______ and jam,

_______ and jam in _______.

Write a sentence using some "short" **ea** words.

____

Activity Sheet 57

Steps to heaven (ea and e)

Name ______________________

Write ten **ea** and ten **e** words on the right ladder.

Write a sentence using some **ea** or **e** words.

____

____

The Day the Zoo Escaped (ly)

Activity Sheet 58

Name ______________________________

Write. ly ______________________________

Fill in the gaps with **ly** words.

The day the zoo escaped
the zebras zipped out __________,
the snakes slid out __________,
the lions marched out __________,
the hyenas laughed out __________,
the mice skipped out __________,
the parrots flew out __________,
but the hippopotamus
stubbornly,
just stayed where it was.

Write a sentence using a **ly** word.

____

____

Activity Sheet 59

Ness (suffix)

Name ______________________________

Write about Glad Ness.

Use as many **ness** words as you can.

Write about Sad Ness.

Use as many **ness** words as you can.

Ness (suffix)

Activity Sheet 60

Name ______________________________

Write about Small Ness.

Use as many **ness** words as you can.

Write about Bright Ness.

Use as many **ness** words as you can.

Activity Sheet 61

Ear! Ear!

Name ______________________________

Choose the best **ear** word to fill the gap.

ear hear dear near fear
nearer clearly tears heard
earth bear heart

I put my ________ to the ________ and what did I ________? I ________ a ________ coming ________!
My ________ went bang, bang, bang. I was shaking with ________.

"Oh ________, oh ________, oh ________!" I said to myself.

I ________ the ________ coming ________ and ________, ________ and ________. I could see it ________ now and I could ________ its growls. It was licking its lips. I burst into ________.

"Don't hurt me ________ ________!" I begged.
The ________ sat down on the ________ ________ to me. It opened its huge mouth and ... it ate my picnic.